Simon Woodroffe launched YO! Sushi in London's Soho in Fe with the banner headline, *"World's Largest Conveyor Belt Sus* there were only a handful of such things outside Japan and anyway most people hadn't even heard of them.

Since then Sushi has taken a firm grip on the world and so has YO! Simon, who knew nothing about restaurants and not a lot about sushi except that he liked it, won awards while YO! was still a small company, albeit always with big ambitions.

It did no harm that Microsoft made a TV commercial about Simon & YO! which was broadcast all over the world. So did American Express, and TV and press coverage has ranged from national news in Japan to the *New York Times* and *The Jewish Chronicle*.

Simon lives alone in London's West End without a TV set and with his own karaoke machine. He rides horses with his daughter Charlotte and her mum, climbs up and skis down mountains and dreams that his tennis will get better.

He reckons that if he had a year left to live, it could be guaranteed that whatever he did would succeed, or if he had unlimited wealth he'd carry on doing what he is doing today: writing, dreaming, scheming, and speaking about YO!.

"Just do it."

Nike

I'd reached the age of 40 in the music and TV business and had some of the biggest names in pop music as my clients. Although it might have seemed to others that I had done OK – I'd had my own businesses – inside I felt frustrated that I had never reached my potential. I wanted to be rich and famous and successful and I felt my time was ticking away. I started writing down my ideas and talking about them and one day a Japanese acquaintance said "What you should do Simon, is a conveyor belt sushi bar with girls in black PVC mini skirts". I'll never forget that – it was a really focused moment. Well, we never did the mini skirts, but those four words "conveyor belt sushi bar" were the catalyst that helped me step into the insecurity of the next few years.

find your destiny.

If I stand in the sand and draw a circle around myself I am in my comfort zone. Now I step outside and I feel fear, and today I know that that is a good place to be. When I stay there for a while I become familiar and the fear subsides. Now I can draw a wider circle around myself and my comfort zone gets larger.

Stepping up to fear:

◆ See how that voice in your head exaggerates the terrors that might befall you.

◆ Write down what that voice is saying and start a training programme to reassure it. The peace that people talk about is when you can get that voice to quieten down.

◆ Make a list of the worst things that could possibly happen – you may find out that it is not as bad as you thought and you won't actually have to go back and live with your mum.

◆ Notice how fear is a physical feeling, and what parts of your body it affects; become an amused observer of your feelings.

◆ Make the subject an everyday and easy part of your conversation.

I never met a person

a dream and regrette

In the late 80s I worked in the TV business selling the rights to music shows and events to broadcasters around the world. I missed the creativity I'd had in the music business, of having an original idea and seeing it come to fruition. I was just a dealmaker for other peoples' work, but I was earning good money so felt trapped. I started writing down ideas for what I could do as an original business. It felt scary to walk away from something safe and face the possibility of losing everything, even if it was potentially very lucrative. As I worked more on

"And the trouble is, if you don't risk anything, you risk even more."

Erica Jong, author of *Fear of Flying*

the possibilities, I started to realise that actually it was even more scary to stay where I was and become unhappy and frustrated and not to fulfil what I thought was my potential. I was creating more and more leverage on myself so that I had to move on. Finally I burnt my bridges by selling a property I had so that I had cash to live on and could give up my remaining consulting work. The pressure was on... I had money to last a year. I cut my expenses right down and got on with it. Eventually it turned into two years. I survived and it became two incredibly happy and fulfilling years, albeit somewhat insecure financially!

...ho gave up financial security to follow
...regardless of subsequent success or failure.

Everyone I have ever met who had the courage to do what they really wanted, believed in hindsight that they had made the right decision. What flows from that decision is an optimism and energy often unimagined and a capacity to work hard. I am fundamentally lazy and I suspect most people are, but when I am doing something I really enjoy I can't stop. Starting a business or making a big life change requires long hours and I can do that when I am loving it. The hard bit is finding what it is that you love.

Finding the way:

◆ Practice removing "I don't know" from your vocabulary and when you are unsure, ask yourself the question, "If I did know the answer what would it be?"

◆ Write down what you'd do if you had a year left to live.

◆ Keep a notebook of all your ideas, yes even the stupid, passing or fleeting ones. Become obsessed with getting them down, even keeping pen and pencil by your bed.

◆ Write down what you'd do if you had a guarantee that whatever you did would succeed.

◆ Consider that often the path lies very close by and that you need only the skills and knowledge you already have, or simply a twist of what you already do.

◆ Talk about it........constantly.

"Courage is fear that has said its prayers."

American proverb

Mostly we do difficult things n from the fear of pain, so I try failing will be painful.

When we opened the first YO! Sushi in London's Soho, I signed the contract with the builders before I had the finance in place. That way there was no way back and I knew I just had to get it. By this time I was two years in and had every penny I owned, and more, invested. I've always found it easy to sleep, even when under pressure, but there were quite a few mornings I was up at 4 a.m. In fact I never needed the money – I had Sony, Honda and All Nippon Airways as sponsors and so the world thought I was a big hitter. The builders didn't send their final bills in straight away and our suppliers gave us extended credit, by which time YO! had taken enough cash to pay them.

om the desire for pleasure, but reate leverage on myself so that

I've noticed that entrepreneurs are always talking about their ideas. Their enthusiasm and openness make things happen. Others get caught up in the project – and the entrepreneur then feels big pressure to produce results. Investing also focuses the mind: whether it is in time, a lump of savings or in my case what I thought were some rather expensive phone calls to Japan!

A painful list:

◆ Tell people about your ideas, especially those that might get stolen. It'll scare them off and scare you into getting them done.

◆ Speak to the press about things you are planning. When they publish you will believe them more – so will others.

◆ Make rash commitments to getting something done by a certain time – scary, but when you deliver you'll feel great and people will think you're Superman.

◆ Say "What I really think is" without knowing how you are going to finish the statement. If your mind is relaxed enough a pearl of wisdom will come out.

◆ Remember your brain is an extremely sophisticated machine for making up terrors that aren't going to happen to you.

> **"All you need in this life is ignorance and confidence, and then success is sure."**
>
> Mark Twain

My brain finds it hard to do something big so delude my negative side

After the Japanese guy told me about conveyor belt sushi bars, I rang up the Japanese trade delegation (this was pre-Internet days). I got all these catalogues in the post that gave a step-by-step illustrated account of how to set up your own conveyor belt sushi bar... in English! I found out they'd been going since the 1960s and there were 3,000 of them in Japan. The conversation with myself went something like, "if this is such a great idea why hasn't someone who knows about restaurants done it before?".

As I set out to write the business plan, instead of thinking "I'm going to create the world's largest chain of sushi bars and a retail brand called YO!" I simply thought "I am going to <u>act as if</u> I am someone who is going to do that... no pressure, just an enjoyable fantasizing, acting game, and just for today". Three months of 'todays' later, I had my brain completely convinced that not only was I going to do this, but that it was the best idea ever and would be an enormous success. The rational side of my brain was aware that this could be delusion but the emotional side believed it.

elieve me when I tell it we are going
ften simply "act as if" and knowingly

Do you have a voice in your head that says things like "you can't do that, you don't know anything about it", or "that won't work or somebody would have done it before", or even simply "you're not good enough"? I do, and I have learned that my relationship and conversation with this voice is where success and failure takes place. In fact I reckon when J.C. said "Get behind me Satan" that was what he was talking about. That voice can be wise too and knows a lot about you that you don't.

Who did I act as if I was?

◆ Richard Branson, the Virgin magician, was one – a bit cheeky and devil may care.

◆ Anthony Robbins, the American development guru, who taught me a lot....Mr Enthusiasm.

◆ Tony Hollingsworth, a TV producer I worked with who kept it simple, giggled and worked hard.

◆ Julian Richer, the English hi-fi retailer, who makes business common sense and doesn't use jargon.

◆ Joe Simpson, the mountaineer whose rope got cut but who never gave up.

◆ The Dalai Lama who taught me that nothing really matters anyway, so why worry?

◆ And many, many others.

9

"Go on failing. Go on. Only next time, fail better."
Samuel Beckett, dramatist

I've noticed that mo
myself daily targets t
punch the air, knowir
I am on track.

Thomas Edison

I was short of two things when I started YO! Sushi: money and a location. I remember calling up real-estate agents who must come across aspiring restaurateurs and dreamers every day, so there were times when I was dismissed pretty unceremoniously. I saw site after site and landlord after landlord and at every rejection I reminded myself that this was not about me and I was one step closer to finding my site. (Thank you Manny Davidson, my first landlord – you were right!) I approached my own bank, and was turned down, but there was an assistant manager there who could see what I was doing and as luck would have it, a year later the manager left and my man got promoted and fought my corner. It took another year and many, many more meetings, but I got the loans. (Thanks for putting your neck on the line for me Phillip Brown.)

uccessful people also fail, so I set
il and when I get six in the bag I

Simple formula really…..ask enough girls for a kiss and one will say yes…..but we don't because we think the pain of all those rejections will outweigh the pleasure of the kiss. And it is the same with business – if I am prepared to be turned down, or to fail, and I can get up and keep going knowing that the rejection is not personal, then I will create more chances to score a goal.

Practise failing:

- Ask someone out with the intention of being rejected…….you might be surprised.

- Make the hardest call you can imagine, after that the others will be easy.

- Tell someone who deserves it how much you love them.

- Score yourself on targets you fail at.

- Tell your boss the thing you have been holding back on (yes….that one!)

- Support and encourage others to fail around you.

"Why, sometimes I've believed as many as six impossible things before breakfast."
Lewis Carroll, *Through the Looking Glass*

At YO! Sushi there are five coloured plates which indicate the price of the food on them. So by eating off the low-cost blues and greens you can economise, or you can go crazy and stack up the pinks and purples. Our price boards used to be magnetic so we could change prices; now they are digital so prices can be changed immediately. And when we open in financial districts, the price of a plate will vary through the day, directly linked to the number of customers in the line, and you'll be able to buy 'futures'. I'm developing video screen ordering for specials that will be delivered by conveyor belt and bleep at you, and we'll use the same screens for video dining between restaurant locations. All part of our Constant And Never-ending Innovation.

...nstant And Never-ending Innovation.

When I first started working with Sainsbury's, the UK supermarket chain, I found out that they strive to "delight" the customer. That's what I want to do too. But I want to go even further and "blow their minds" by constantly titillating them with new things. You can't create a masterpiece concept anymore and say, "that's it, now we'll roll it out". The 21st century concepts that succeed will be those that continually re-invent themselves, just like Madonna.

Finding ideas:

◆ Allow yourself to fantasise – if you are enjoying it you are in the right place.

◆ Often the really good ideas start out as the whacky ones, so don't dismiss them before they have a chance to mature.

◆ Allow yourself some lazy time, whether it's in the garden, the bathtub or the car. Let your mind loose to fly.

◆ Try behaving out of character or go to a meeting and act as if you are someone you admire.

◆ Go to a supermarket and wander around looking at the shapes with a blank mind.

◆ The most impossible ideas sometimes have the most useful content.

"Well done is quickly done."
Caesar Augustus, 63 B.C. – 14 A.D

Business is a bit lik
couple of seconds

When I first heard about the Millennium Dome I thought it sounded a great place to showcase YO! Sushi to the world. So I approached them and after a large number of phone calls managed to get a meeting. They'd never heard of us so there was a bit of explaining to do, and then I thought I was on my way. It eventually took me a year and a half to get in, after much persistence, including help from my brother who was doing the lighting there, and e-mails copied to Ministers of State (who knows what went on behind the scenes, but it was exciting as I pressed the send button each time!). When we did get agreement, they were very welcoming and in spite of the later bad publicity, the build-up and the opening were a great experience. Most of the rest of the caterers were much larger organisation than us but we got great reviews and became a bit of a minor celeb in there. The numbers never really made it a great commercial decision but I learned a lot, especially that if you simply never give up, you nearly always get it (although it may not always be what you had anticipated).

ɔrmula One motor racing... I'm gaining a
p, but one mistake and the guy behind is through.

People worry that the world is changing so quickly, but that is what makes it so exciting. There has never been an easier time to get into business and challenge the bigger boys. Nobody can sit on their laurels, and small organisations can change faster than larger ones.

Travelling at speed:

◆ I try to take and return calls quickly. Sifting through messages left three times and eventually calling back wastes time on something that could have been dealt with immediately. People like it too.

◆ Make quick decisions. The occasional bad one is easily outweighed by the benefits of making more decisions more quickly.

◆ While I strive for perfection, I am willing to compromise not 10 but 20 or 30 or 40 per cent in order to make something happen immediately.

◆ Delegate upwards as well as downwards and sideways – searching for shortcuts.

◆ Busy…ness is a state of mind – when a busy person gives me their time, I feel like a million dollars.

◆ Take time in your busy day to give someone's small problem your big attention.

When I was opening my first restaurant I went out looking for sponsors. I liked the people at Sony Consumer Products. I never gave up for a year. I never asked for too much and never put them under any pressure. With no contract of any sort they delivered some TVs and sound equipment two weeks before we opened (I had some equipment on hold just in case – it was that close). I later found out that they get 100 requests a week, virtually none of which get through. The same happened with Honda who lent me a

"Perseverance is failing 19 times and succeeding the 20th."

Julie Andrews, who climbed a few mountains herself

delivery bike and All Nippon Airways who gave me some upgrades to Japan. I never asked Honda for much and told them that I was so grateful that not only would I promote them in the restaurant but that they would be on everything as official sponsors ... and that if they didn't reply within a week I would assume that they had agreed. Of course they didn't reply, so I put them up everywhere and on all the press releases. And when we opened everybody asked "who is this guy Simon Woodroffe? He's got these Japanese giants behind him". Of course they didn't give us much but it was a big deal to have their names!

n't try to get them to say t to say 'No'.

I call it the Seven Meeting Rule and my experience is that once you have invested that much time with someone, something will happen......if someone persists enough with me and the experience is good, I'll usually give in if they can keep me going long enough.

Avoiding no:

- ◆ Go around stone walls – or ignore them.

- ◆ Go back up what you thought were blind alleys. Sometimes you just missed the exit first time round.

- ◆ Expose ploys, especially your own.

- ◆ Give more than they could ever dream of.

- ◆ Build golden bridges that make it easy for people to walk towards you.

- ◆ Leave silences – that way you'll hear what's going on.

"Love your family"
Charlotte Woodroffe. YO! T-shirt.

I can change my behavio
change yours in a lifetim

I got divorced in my late 30s and it threw me to me knees. For the first time I thought to myself that maybe a few, just a few, of my problems are of my own making, and nothing to do with other people or circumstances. Sounds trite, but it was a great realisation for me because I could start looking at my part in every single situation. I'd always had friends who visited the Alcoholics Anonymous programme and, although I didn't qualify for membership, I'd been to observe some of their meetings and was impressed. I learned that by listening carefully I could understand much better what was going on with others and myself, and that within myself was an enormous wisdom that already knew most of the answers if I could only tune in to them. I also realised that my excuses and justifications and blame only served as barriers to achieving what I wanted. They were "rackets" that I had skillfully built around me to justify why I couldn't do this or that.

a heartbeat but I'll never

If I'm in a conflict and it is 90 per cent your fault and just 10 per cent mine, I know I can't change what you do, but I can create a 10 per cent shift in the situation by changing my part. This often works wonders.

Conflict:

◆ What are the "rackets" that stop you moving forward?

◆ Create a systematic search – you are especially looking for the things that "you don't know that you don't know".

◆ When you get to "I don't know" ask, "What would the answer be if I did know?" (It's a great line to use with someone else too!)

◆ You already know all the answers, if only you'd listen to yourself. This is just as true for business decisions as for emotional change.

◆ When you get a parking ticket you can get over it immediately or spend an hour, a day or a week being angry about the injustice of it. The person who gets hurt if you prolong it is you.

> **"The journey of a thousand miles starts with one step."**
> Chairman Mao

The period of my life prior to starting YO! Sushi was spent in the TV business and I was unhappy because I had not fulfilled my potential. At twenty my plan had been to be a millionaire by thirty, at thirty it had become thirty-five, and so on. Time was ticking away and I was procrastinating. A big change came when I learned about writing down goals. I divided them into Home, Career and Health and got them down on paper, revisiting them every day to refine and shorten them. I was creating strong statements that were like a tune you cannot get out of your head. I actually got them laminated and 'rapped' my spoken goals to a karaoke backing track. For Career I used The Beatles' "Eight Days a Week" and for Home, Jan and Dean singing "Two Girls for Every Boy". It was enormously powerful and, having walked around the park with it on the Walkman, within three weeks I was running four miles – beyond my wildest dreams of fitness. I felt like Superman...if I could handle this I could do anything!

ecomes a hundred per cent in three months.

Sometimes when I look at the mountain to climb it seems overwhelming. When I chip away a little bit at a time, I am surprised at how quickly the pile is reduced. Often the items on my list that I keep putting off have simple solutions when I summon the will to deal with them.

Creating change:

◆ What would you do if it could be guaranteed that whatever you did would succeed spectacularly?

◆ What would you do if you were given just a year of healthy life to live. Scary but focusing.

◆ Repetition is powerful. If you want to run, start by walking short distances but do it in a routine.

◆ Do it now...yes that means right now...just a tiny bit...to get it started.

◆ Talk about it. As you talk about it, you talk yourself into it.

◆ Don't beat yourself up...this is the big one...to succeed you have to fail so be happy with your failures.

"The best way to invent the future is to predict it."
Alan Kay, father of the laptop computer

I like to imagine the futu
present with the benefit

I left school at the end of the 60s in the days when we used to do peace signs and mean them. After a couple of halcyon years I realised that my father was right and that having a job oiled the wheels of life. I liked Rock'n'Roll so I started off as a roadie putting up the lights. I used to tell the bands that we should do to the shows what Busby Berkeley did to the movies in the 1930s and eventually, completely untrained, I became a stage designer. I could imagine wild extravaganzas, but at that time Rock'n'Roll didn't want that and the technology didn't exist to create it. So I bided my time, imagining how it could be, and always trying to do more. Eventually the Rock'n'Roll spectacle came of age and I was there designing some of the great shows. People ask me today "Don't you miss show-business?" And of course I say, "I'm still in it".

d from there, look back at the agined hindsight.

Linda McCartney said, "why would you want to eat something that had a face?" And I think that when mankind looks back at us 100 years hence, they will see meat eaters (including me) as barbaric. Food production will be revolutionised during that time so that the taste and textures of grown food will be more desirable than eating animals and thus will come the change.

Imagined hindsight:

◆ A system called "commuting" was once prevalent where workers travelled from their sleeping homes to their working homes every day!

◆ It was once believed that telepathy and mind-reading were supernatural phenomena – in the days before mind-mail replaced e-mail.

◆ When hundreds of millions of people were starving, people still fought against GM food delaying the food revolution of today.

◆ The invention of ART (automatic real-time language translation) was the single most important factor in the elimination of war.

◆ As recently as the 21st century, people shopped in supermarkets where odd-shaped boxes were packed in plastic bags and carried home.

I had a call one day in 1998. "This is Microsoft's advertising agency", the American voice said, "and we'd like to test you for a TV commercial". "Come on, who's that?" I said, thinking I was being wound up, but it was true, and they went ahead and made a 30 second TV commercial that went out all over the world. American Express featured YO! Sushi in a TV commercial as well. Those ads probably cost more to show than YO! had ever taken. The power of TV sowed the seed of YO! in countless minds around the world and if we water and care for that seed it will grow.

"The harder I practise, the luckier I get."
Gary Player

e world conspires to support you in
ever have believed possible.

Given the chance meetings and happy coincidences that happen to me I often wonder about the "near misses" – there must be hundreds of them. My neighbour met someone she had had a holiday romance with 10 years ago and found out that the person had been living in an apartment she could see from her kitchen window. The world is a complex web that cannot be unravelled in one or a hundred lifetimes, but underlying it are natural orders and the statement above is one of them.

Some things that happened:

◆ After committing to the name I discovered that "Yo" is the greeting between men in Japan.

◆ The YO! logo as drawn reads "Japanese" in Hebrew, if you squint a little.

◆ I intended to open in Soho. When the building was sold to someone else, I fought for a year and won it from five competitors all with better finances than mine.

◆ Sony Consumer Products gave me valuable sound and video equipment with no contractual obligations.

◆ 4i, the design company, developed the brand identity and never charged me a penny until I could afford it.

◆ I was given state-of-the-art lighting worth $100,000 as a test site.

25

"One machine can do the work of fifty ordinary men. No machine can do the work of one extraordinary man."

Elbert G Hubbard, writer and businessman (1856-1915)

I like to work wi
positive revoluti

I went to visit a food supplier recently and on arriving found a solid looking sign in the prime parking space "Reserved for Simon Woodroffe" it said. I was welcomed warmly at reception and they even knew in advance how I took my coffee. I felt important, respected, honoured even. It felt very good and as a result the meeting got off to an excellent start and we concluded our deal. Later I commended the factory manager on the welcome and he told me that soon after the receptionist who had been responsible for my welcome started there, she approached him and asked for a change of job title. She wanted to be a technologist like the factory staff. "What sort?" the manager asked. "An F.I.T." she said. "What's an F.I.T.?" he asked. "A First Impressions Technologist", she told him. That's what I call a revolutionary. This lady had figured out how she could really make a difference, and was ready to communicate her enthusiasm for that in a powerful way.

Mahatma Gandhi

volutionaries. The world is in a
d those people understand.

radical journe

nostalgic jour

Getting things to actually happen, creating change, generating new revenue, figuring out what will make the biggest difference to customers, profitability or the company's well-being. These are the sort of things that the people I call revolutionaries want. They want to make a difference and are willing to take risks to do what their instincts tell them are good ideas. Dynamic companies applaud revolutionaries and create an environment in which they can succeed.

Revolutionaries

◆ Play the detective when taking up references, you'll learn more from that than from hours of interviews.

◆ Revolutionaries like to be leaders, creating new divisions, companies or accounting structures so they can run their own show.

◆ Allow people to write their own job descriptions, they know what they can and would like to do better than you do.

◆ When it's right, I can work all night. And when it's not, I'll get nothing done in days.

◆ Challenge people to tell you what they should do, and then let them do it.

Meat Loaf – Bat out of Hell tour

I started my first company designing stages at the age of 25 as a part-owned subsidiary of a large lighting company. It was a fairly safe way to get going and when the lighting company got into financial trouble a few years later I had some loyal clients like Rod Stewart and The Moody Blues who came with me to the partnership I then formed. At least I like to think they were loyal, but they probably didn't have much choice as we were halfway through producing their shows! My third company was in the TV business with some Americans. At least I thought it was my company, but the only "like-mindedness" about us was that we all thought it was our company! So I learned that business partnerships are like marriages. After two "divorces" I figured that I might be better on my own and that is what I did in my final years in TV. Actually I learned that, as with any relationship, it is more important to like the people you are in business with than to need them. That's when I started YO! Sushi.

**"You have achieved excellence as a leader
when people will follow you anywhere, if only
out of curiosity!"**
General Colin Powell

s in a group of like-minded people.

When I was young I read Arthur Conan Doyle's *The White Company* about a group of adventurers who rode around old England. I have always seen the word "company" this way. When a group of people are enjoying the same mission, quantum leaps in achievement can happen.

Questioning your company:

◆ They used to call me the steam roller – what would your nickname be?

◆ If you were in business would you be a "go-it-aloner" or a "sharer with others" and why?

◆ Can you let go? When people you work with make mistakes how do you react?

◆ Ask the people you work with what they think you'll be doing 5 or 10 years from now.

◆ Then ask them what they think you could be doing if you were really to fly.

◆ What advice would you give yourself if "yourself" asked you?

"The situation is desperate but not serious."

Irish rugby team manager during a disastrous season

I am serious about m
I don't give a damn!

If there is one thing I have learned about myself it is that when it all becomes too important, then it is stressful. And then I alienate people and make bad decisions. Which is why I used to be called the Steam Roller. Until I worked out what was the worst thing that could happen, which was that I'd run out of money and I'd have to go back and live with my mum. And even that wouldn't be so bad because she's quite nice, my mum (well actually it wouldn't be that great even though she is nice). So the picture I have as I go through my workaday life is that on one shoulder I have this serious bloke who works incredibly hard and is organised and wants everything done efficiently and immediately. And on the other shoulder I have this giggling character who asks "how could you be so serious?" and "most of the time it won't happen how you want it anyway, so why are you getting so wound up?". And one side balances the other, so most of the time I don't get stressed and I make good decisions and retain my friends. Most of the time.

I have noticed that all of the philosophical religions are sympathetic to notions of 'destiny' or 'fate' or 'God's will'. I think this is a very good ploy because when we truly believe that 'whatever will be will be' then off comes the pressure and we shrug and allow things to happen as they will. That doesn't mean that we don't try incredibly hard; it just means that we accept the results as they are handed out.

Dealing with stress:

- Practise recognising pressure and labelling it with your own words.

- Breathe deeply and slowly, and stop trying to solve the problem.

- Activate "I don't care" even if you really do!

- Learn to giggle.

- Get off the case. Get on with something else. Go away.

- Help someone with a problem smaller than yours.

- Giggle some more.

"Feel the fear and do it anyway."
Susan Jeffers

The four human emotions are

After my divorce and my realisation that there were character defects that stood between me and the happiness I sought, I set out to find the things about myself that "you don't know that you don't know" as someone put it. For example, I never thought that I was an angry person and I discovered that although I covered it up well I was actually a walking stick of dynamite. If somebody messed something up or crossed me, I was a 'putter-downer'. "How could you possibly do or think that?", I'd imply, even if I didn't say it in so many words. I started off seeing a Jungian analyst who taught me about my dreams. I had my own therapist for a while and I did quite a few of the personal development courses including a really heavyweight one in America where we danced around in the woods in various forms of dress or undress. I never gave away my power of decision but I did learn to trust some good teachers and I learned a lot. I also managed to retain a sense of humour (most of the time) and avoided the psychobabble!

Carl Gustav Jung

nger, Sadness, Happiness and Fear.

They can be remembered as Mad, Sad, Glad and Scared and every human feeling falls into one of these categories. At any one time we are experiencing one or more of these and sometimes all of them at once. The best way to find out which one is to check the feeling in your body.

Feeling:

◆ Think about the things that you don't know that you don't know about yourself.

◆ Your own sadness is commonly the most difficult emotion to be in touch with. Are you aware of yours?

◆ Consider what freefloating anger you carry in your body. Road rage, for example, is never about driving.

◆ Fear is probably the most common human emotion, which is why so much is written about it and why it is on the first page of this book.

◆ If you're not doing what you want to, consider that somewhere in the fear category is the thing that stops you being the person you'd like to be.

◆ When you are happy, enjoy it!

" **While you're chuckling at the list on the other page, consider how people may chuckle at us in the next century."**

Simon Woodroffe

We tend to overestima[t]
and underestimate wha[t]

If I'd opened YO! Sushi at the end of the first development year it would not have been half what it is today. At the time I was thinking how we could serve drinks in a more useful way and I'd come up with motorised trolleys on rails, but I was worried about ladies heels getting stuck in the tracks. Then I thought "robots"(isn't that a great word) but where to get them? I'd heard that if you were a big company you could call up the universities for help. Here's a chance to fail I thought and I tried Loughborough University in the English Midlands telling them my story. "Try Edinburgh," they said and gave me a number, and guess what? The phone rang and was answered with the immortal words "Robot Department – how can I help you?" Well three hours later I was speaking to Martin who had developed a system for robotic wheelchairs and was willing to help me. A few weeks before we opened I saw a robot drinks trolley go round a corner unaided and speaking too: "move your fat arse, some of us have a fucking job to do round here," it said, and I thought to myself that at least people were going to come in and have a look. Only a robot could be rude to a customer and get away with it!

hat will happen in the next two years ill happen in the next ten.

The future is invented in the minds of men, so we already know what is going to happen. Remember those comics you read as children; now you're grown up and all those things you read about like computers and monorails and robots have come true. It took longer than we imagined and the next future has already been written.

Predictions:

- "Heavier-than-air flying machines are impossible." **Lord Kelvin,** *Royal Society President 1895*

- "Everything that can be invented has been invented." **Charles Duell,** *US Office of Patents 1895*

- "I think there is a world market for maybe five computers." **Thomas Watson,** *IBM Chairman 1943*

- "Computers in the future may weigh no more than 1.5 tons." Popular Mechanics *magazine 1949*

- "We don't like their sound, and guitar music is on the way out." *Decca records rejecting The Beatles 1962*

- "640K ought to be enough for anyone." **Bill Gates** *1981*

To develop new concep
committees don't cut it.

If I'd gone out to market research conveyor belt sushi bars with robots before I opened YO! Sushi, the results would have been: "what is the guy talking about?" To begin with a lot of people in London didn't know that they liked sushi. It was only when they got tempted in by all the fun, and discovered there was lots to eat as well as raw fish, that they decided "this sushi stuff is pretty good". Same as when I launched massage in YO! Below. Everybody said, "you can't massage people in a bar when they've been drinking" and if we'd been a committee or large company the idea would've been thrown right out. But I knew that the way to find out was to try it, and because all my team were into it they found ways to deal with the problems. What better way I say to get close to your customers than to rub oil on their naked shoulders!

"Search all of your parks in all of your cities and you will not find a statue of a committee."
David Ogilvy, advertising guru

quires individuals and time...

Committees and market research produce mediocrity, so often it is one person's obsession that can break truly new ground: Edison and the light bulb, Dyson and the bagless vacuum cleaner. Development takes time to go up the wrong paths and to refine, refine, refine.

◆ Sometimes it is better to get it right...time creates quality.

◆ Give people time and money for pet projects.

◆ You can't market research what a market doesn't know about.

◆ Demand failure for your people, put it in their objectives.

◆ Do outrageous things – it gets you noticed.

◆ If you can't do something because it's against the rules, change the rules.

> **"Making money is art and working is art and good business the best art of all."**
> Andy Warhol

I am not exceptionally intelligent. Add to that no academic training and a tendency toward laziness if I'm not enjoying it, and it does not add up to a lot. But over a period of time I have built up an instinct as to what works, what will and won't happen, and often I can spot opportunities and I'm willing to run with them. Designing stages for rock bands exposed me to working with brands, which they are, every bit as much as YO! or Coca-Cola are. And I also learned that the experience of being young all over the world is a very similar experience, albeit set in different cultures. Having small companies taught me that there is really only one rule that leads to potential success and that is "don't run out of cash...especially near payday". Access to great financial information is paramount. You can have a very popular well-known product and make zilch out of it or you can make fortunes out of a corner shop. Controlling your margins is everything.

...pecially financial ones.

The dictionary defines intelligence as the ability to grasp concepts. A great brain for me is one that can see the way ahead and puts values on what is important and what is not. It collects all that myriad of information and sifts it into a cohesive plan.

Margin calls:

◆ Everything else being equal, a high margin business is better than a low margin business.

◆ Even if everything is not equal, then higher margin is better.

◆ Accountants are creatives too.

◆ Creativity and conservatism equals financial prudence.

◆ Cashflow is a life support system.

"I did it my way."
Frank Sinatra and Sid Vicious

Every family has its own wa

The company that made the Microsoft TV commercial was Wieden & Kennedy. I found out they are one of the world's most successful agencies; for example they were behind all the great Nike advertising. But instead of being located on Madison Avenue they chose Portland, Oregon where they have built a groundbreaking building. Their culture allows individuals to be themselves and flourish and the people who work there are often best friends. So they are all doing what they love with people they like and they are very, very successful and make lots of money too. I think customers recognise their integrity and like them for it, as well as the creative flair it encourages. One of their traditions is "Founders Day" when Dan Wieden and Dave Kennedy host a day of celebration for everyone. I visited them on that day and it felt like the last day of term at school and Christmas and Thanksgiving all rolled into one. Everybody had been anticipating it for weeks and the power of this family coming together felt enormous, and glued them together during the next year.

f doing Christmas.

So you get married and the first Christmas comes around and how do you do it? Is Christmas dinner in the middle of the day or the evening. Do you have presents before or after the meal? We all have different backgrounds and perceptions about how things should be done. Building up traditions of how your group or family or company does things is enormously powerful, and people love the feeling of belonging that this brings.

Ritual power:

◆ Research what traditions other companies or groups have – the more whacky the better.

◆ Try changing a routine.

◆ Ask the questions, "Am I doing this because I always have? Is there another way to do this?"

◆ Get out of your comfort zone and take a leap of faith to do something someone else's way.

◆ A tradition is just a good idea that sticks. Find some.

◆ Look at how somebody else does what you do, and what they do better (be honest).

◆ Set your workforce free (dress-down Friday is just parole).

"Then I'll sue you for using brothers in Warner Brothers."

Groucho Marx when told that Warner Brothers, who had just released "Casablanca", objected to the Marx Brothers using the title "A Night in Casablanca".

I hope that one day we'll look back and say that YO! was always destined to be an international retail brand and that it just happened to be a sushi bar in its first manifestation. After the name was chosen I found out that "yo" is the formal greeting between men in Japan, and the logo looks like the character for the word "Japanese" in Hebrew script. WOW! Graham and Mark from 4i, our designers, mocked up the logo first time against a background of a Japanese street scene and it looked great. We showed some Japanese people and wondered why they were looking at us strangely until we found out the picture was of a red light district! When I started the sushi delivery service it just had to be called YO! to GO and our first bar which was on the lower floor of YO! Sushi got called YO! Below. Then merchandise for children called Baby YO! and YO! You Kids felt good and the hotel concept YOTEL! and grocery brand YOGANIC! followed. "This works," I thought, and when the *Times* newspaper asked me what next, a naughty thought crept into my head. I described the smoke-extracting ashtrays we have in YO! Below and told the journalist that when marijuana is legalised we'd extract all the smoke into a special room and charge people to go in and call it "YO! to Blow". "YO! goes to Pot" was the headline (and they thought I was joking).

What's in a name?

The Beatles wasn't the greatest name but became the most famous one in pop history. Hoover became an English language word and it drives James Dyson crazy when people use it about his superior vacuum cleaner. Virgin was a great name because at the time of its inception, it was very cheeky. You can get to be famous without a great name. But having one helps.

Great names:

- The Grateful Dead
- The Oscars
- Sony Walkman
- EasyJet and EasyEverything
- Wagamama
- Star Wars
- Smart Car
- Madonna
- Sergeant Pepper's Lonely Hearts Club Band

"We are the World"
USA for Africa

The experience of being youn‹

In the 1970s, the rock shows I designed toured the world and I saw the same audiences having the same experiences, drinking the same drinks and eating the same burgers. The last show my design and staging company was involved in was Live Aid, which was a visible portrayal of that world youth culture. Later as a businessman selling the TV rights to live broadcasts like the Nelson Mandela shows or concerts by Elton John, Billy Joel or Genesis, I travelled the world seeing how music, TV and film created a youth culture that broke away from thousand year-old domestic cultures, and let youth stand proudly and together. Today, for the first time there is a truly international commercial culture around the world, and only the companies that can command international respect will truly succeed. YO! will have to reach out across the world and across cultures, in the same way as the Beatles or The Rolling Stones did.

a similar one around the world.

Whether you live in Moscow, Madrid or Moosedroppings, Iowa, young people grow up in an international popular culture as well as in their own historical culture. Pop culture extends from movies to music, from sport to just chatting, and is communicated through TV, media and the Internet. Communication is what the Internet was invented for, not marketing and selling. I look forward to a day when loyalties and relationships are to like-minded communities rather than geographical locations, and these communities span the planet bringing us ever closer as human beings.

It's a changing world:

◆ Most Manchester United supporters do not even live in England, never mind Manchester.

◆ Children in Scandinavian schools speak English in the playground.

◆ Sushi outsells the most popular British sandwich in Glasgow, Scotland.

◆ Amazon.com can deliver 13 million books anywhere in the world.

◆ McDonald's opens a new restaurant every day somewhere in the world.

◆ Coca-Cola has the world's largest transport fleet.

◆ OK is the world's most universally understood word.

Peter Sellers as Inspector Clouseau on finding the other detective hiding in a hotel wardrobe

"Ahh... the old cupboard ploy"

Peter Sellers as Inspector Clouseau

When I first went to Japan at the beginning of the 90s, it was for a live TV broadcast by Jon Bon Jovi and an unlikely mix of traditional Japanese musicians playing with artists like Bob Dylan and INXS. I noticed that in meetings the Japanese spent a great deal of time on the formalities of introduction and small talk, all done with a great deal of respect. And by the time these rituals were complete, the business of the day could get done very quickly because everybody felt comfortable and on the same wavelength – part of what they call "nemawashi". I had always been short and to the point in meetings, wanting to achieve the results immediately. So I started to experiment with letting go a bit and enjoying the people and the process. In fact I went so far that I banned myself from using any business-speak at all and trying to find simplistic and naïve views of situations. I learned a great deal, and my experience is that the human and open approach works the best. As we sit around a table and talk – business or otherwise – we are gifted as human beings as arch-manipulators. Even in truly healthy and loving relationships this happens and everybody has his or her ploys. So to expose ploys, my own and those of others, brings a truthfulness that creates trust and resolution.

uch the human being.

Most of the successful people I have met have a talent for connecting with others at a very human level. That is not to say that they are necessarily charming or amusing, but that there is a sense of knowing who the person is. When somebody tells me something directly, even though I may not like it, I trust them because I know where I stand.

- Mirror the body language of the people you are with to create rapport.
- Search for simple homely words.
- Immediately seek clarification on any buzzword.
- Use superlatives sparingly.
- Write letters with fewer words.
- Kiss often.... (Keep It Simple Stupid).

"The Beatles are more popular than Jesus."

John Lennon

I never set out to build a brand and I have my suspicions of any advertising agency or designer who does. What a brand should do is to reflect the true spirit of the group of people it represents and communicate that spirit truthfully to the world. Without truth and substance beneath, brand can only be gloss and will not survive. The Rolling Stones tongue is a reflection of the lead vocalist's anatomy and the band's attitude. McDonald's golden arches reflected the pioneering spirit of the company as it emerged in the 1950s, and the TGI Friday's character spills out through its waiters, in a tradition that is handed down in their exemplary training. YO! is an exhilarating exclamation of life and celebrates an optimism for the future in a changing world. There has always been an enthusiasm and excitement in our company. People ask how we will keep that as we grow larger. I don't know, but I do know that I will enjoy watching its growth. The other question I get asked is why we build brand extensions like YOTEL! and YOGANIC! when their failure might reflect badly on the existing operation. Well, it seems to me that there is no need to climb the mountain twice. The YO! name has power, so I should use it. I can cope with the occasional tumble. In fact done openly it could be quite endearing (why don't politicians learn that?).

nd how not to build the mountain twice.

We don't build emotional attachments to banks, but we do to film stars and singers. A child will resist eating something new, but wrap it up in a familiar wrapper and they'll try it. As adults we seek things we can trust and stick with them until proven wrong.

Brands people love:

◆ Harley-Davidson. People tattoo this brand on their bodies.

◆ Mickey Mouse, endearing us to Disney

◆ The Bible. Or any book of truth.

◆ Marilyn Monroe, James Dean, Hendrix.... fill in your own icon.

◆ Happy Meal toys are sold as collector's items.

◆ VW Beetles for over 50 years.

"You can observe a lot just by watching."

Yogi Berra, baseball manager and player

Yogi Berra

The greatest insights I have ever had into myself and other human beings, (and in spite of being a climber and a sailor, some of the greatest adventures too) have been in group therapy. Because however much I learn by speaking myself, being able to listen to another person who feels safe and secure being open about their feelings in a situation where there are no interruptions makes me realise two things. Firstly, people are incredibly similar and over the period of a lifetime have mostly the same emotional experiences to a greater or lesser degree. And secondly, by listening attentively and watching you can recognise that humanity in others on a daily basis. I remember being with a man who I had always thought of as arrogant and overbearing, until he told a story that when he swaggered into the bar full of bravado and bonhomie, he actually felt like a little kid who wasn't really grown up enough to be there. I remember thinking that there were probably one or two more in that bar feeling the same way. I always wanted to be part of the "In" crowd too, and would gravitate to whoever I thought was the hippest person there. I know today that when I give my time to someone who is perhaps a little less secure, the need to compete slips away and I feel good.

50

like wearing mental X-ray specs.

When someone is talking to me, if I can quieten my mind down, listen attentively, leave a gap at the end of their words and leave off thinking of my own response until then…then I learn a great deal about them and I command their attention when I speak.

Positive manipulation:

- All human beings experience the same fundamental feelings.

- By empathising with another person, you are better able to influence them.

- Be aware of how you influence others. There's nothing wrong with positive manipulation.

- Leave long silences… consider your own words and those of others… it's powerful.

- Spend some of your time with the underdog or the one who is "left out".

- Wear great clothes – it works – you'll find more people listen to you.

"The problem in America today is not that we fail, it is that we don't risk failing enough."

Philip Knight of Nike

After Live Aid my old business partner went off to live in New York and I took on the office overhead in London in a dejected state personally and lacking in confidence. I felt that the design business in Rock 'n Roll had grown up and I was out of my depth. In fact I felt as if I had always been a bit of a scammer, having had no formal training, and that I'd got found out. But I had learned that when you hit a crisis if you blow the problem up out of proportion you can see it clearly and you can deal with it there and then before it comes back and slaps you in the face. (Now don't tell me that you don't know what your problem is or even what the answer may be. I am telling you that you almost certainly do know, and in a great deal of detail, if you find the courage and discipline to address it. The trouble usually is that addressing it is painful, and keeping your head in the sand and hoping is easier). Anyway within a week I'd made a decision and spent real and dwindling money on redecoration and partitioning. I let out all my office, except a corner for me (one of the first serviced-office lettings) and I let my secretary and draughtsman go. Immediately I was actually cash positive with time to think and explore my future.

All businesses can be hit by a crisis, whether due to the activities of a competitor or economic change or even the boss's personal circumstances. Unless you're very lucky you don't have surplus profits sloshing around waiting for that rainy day. It's really just like your finances at home – if you hit hard times the smart guy cuts right back on his spending or drops his price for odd jobs. Companies that can move and change the fastest are the ones that feel the safest.

Safety first:

◆ When you have an inkling about a problem, exaggerate it in your mind and deal with it early.

◆ Plan for those possible crises you already know could happen – job loss, recession, interest rate changes, competitors and in my case a fish scare!

◆ Insure loss of profits in the case of fire or flood, for at least two years, preferably three. Someone who survived that calamity told me he could have bought any competitor he wished if he had been insured.

◆ In the good times, plan for the bad times by talking to your colleagues about what might be the unseen problems ahead. It'll focus your thinking before you take on more overhead.

◆ Put a "dynamic" fund , however small, into a separate account and be prepared to deal with problems when they are still small.

"Change is inevitable, except from a vending machine."
Graffiti

In the first summer after we opened YO! Sushi I was asked to do four seminars on a cruise ship for a catering forum. Sounds great, I thought, and when I saw pictures of my cabin suite it felt even greater. But I was quite nervous because I hadn't done any public speaking previously. So I set up a series of seminars with people within the company, and at each one I tried out a different format. I found out that what worked best was when I said what I was thinking and feeling rather than cleverly constructed arguments. When I lost my place or got stuck as a seminar leader it could be endearing rather than embarrassing. If I asked the audience for help immediately rather than bluffing through they warmed to me. And at question time it was more powerful to ask the audience to share their experiences rather than simply answering questions. That's where I learned the technique of saying "What I truly believe is" without knowing what is to follow and then listening to the words in my head to complete the sentence. I also learned to say "what comes to mind is" or "today's answer to that question is".

ou'll get what you've always got.

A great way to succeed is by throwing mud at the wall and hoping that it sticks. But you've got to throw it a different way every time, because if one technique doesn't work however many times you throw it you'll get the same result. And the same goes for business. Keep trying different ways until you hit on a winning formula.

If:

◆ If the tough approach doesn't work, try the sweet one.

◆ If shouting doesn't work, try whispering.

◆ If being subtle doesn't work, try being up front.

◆ If the advertising isn't working, try another publication.

◆ If you don't meet the girl in a bar, look on the sports field.

◆ If you can't talk them into a better price, try walking away.

◆ If they can't get in on time, try locking them out.

"To sing the blues you have to have had them."

Big Joe Williams

The hardest time of my life was the two years it took to get divorced. Once I had gotten over the rejection, the hard part was the unfairness of it all, so I thought. I remember getting the formal letter from the lawyer and tearing it up in my anger. "How could they play this game of reasonableness?" I ranted. "It was my life, my family, my security." The insecurity of it all, what would become of me? And how I suffered with all the injustice. It was only when I started to realise that this was just the way it was, and so what. I wasn't going to change anybody, it was going to happen how it was going to happen anyway. So I might as well get on with it and do the best I could do. And then most likely it would work out OK as everything else always had. So I just started throwing off the resentment and began to understand everyone else's side. I started feeling less pressure and started getting on with what I had to do. When it was all resolved I looked back and wondered what all the worry was about. Human beings are designed to get used to the most uncomfortable situations remarkably quickly... it soon becomes normal.

the greatest truth.

When I truly understand that life is hard and that that is the natural order of things then I stop complaining. So and so is charging me too much, someone will complain. "Well," I'll say, "so would I if I could". Or I'll hear someone moaning on about something. "So life is normal," I'll say, and I'll see their head nod and a smile come on their face… they already know. Most people struggle for quite large amounts of the time; amazing but true. So enjoy when times are good and accept when they are not…it's normal.

Hard times:

- ◆ Wherever you are is where you need to be; it's a learning process.

- ◆ You learn little from the good times, but lots from the bad times.

- ◆ Practise letting go of resentments instantly.

- ◆ Learn to eliminate the word "but" completely from your sentences.

- ◆ Every situation can be improved. The first step is the beginning of a new journey.

- ◆ It's no rehearsal. This is it, yes, today, right now… live your life to the fill-me-up.

The revolution that will happe be a quasi-spiritual revolution.

On my own journey I grew up comparing myself to others and feeling wanting, with work, girls, and other men. I remember as I went through divorce, my brother sending me a letter telling me to "get some help" and angrily tearing it up. "Who do you think I am?" I thought, yet it was that process of self examination that allowed me to break through the things that had held me back and start to become the person I wanted to be and I'm still doing it every day. Who knows what will happen. My life is not a rehearsal. I know that the time is now and the place is here and I am acting on my dreams even as I write this final sentence.

"Life is what happens to you while you're busy making other plans"

John Lennon, musician

You can see the seeds in the growing interest in astrology, the popularity of practices from feng shui to t'ai chi, and the proliferation of self help books and even TV talk shows. What we are all seeking is happiness, and people are realising that the "when I get the job or the money or girlfriend..." approach is a syndrome that will only go on and on. You are already happy and learning to find that happiness in the process of your journey through life is a sweet discovery.

◆ Toast: I once met a punk rocker wearing only a dustbin liner with a piece of toast where his underpants should have been.

◆ Blue: the colour of the sea, the sky, the pale suede Cuban boots I wore in 1970 and my favourite John Pearse shirts.

◆ Morning: getting up early (like 4am). Even in the city, it's fresh, you can smell more, the world belongs to you and the whole day lies ahead.

◆ Mountain: overwhelmingly large, pure, clean, mysterious and full of adventure.

◆ Music: so loud the brain forgets and the body moves, shaking your arms in the sky, all one.

◆ Talking: late, late, the smell of hibiscus rising in the air.

◆ Gentle: my little girl in my arms, loving, full of a life ahead.

**"This is the end,
my only friend,
the end."**

Jim Morrison, The Doors

YO! Sushi is always interested in your opinions, so hit the website and leave us a message or mail us what you think, want, love, hate or would like improved.

You can visit YO! Sushi in the UK

- In the west village of Bluewater shopping centre in Kent, now the world's largest conveyor belt sushi bar.

- Poland Street in Soho which was the first restaurant and is the first YO! Below.

- My hotel in Bedford Square near Tottenham Court Road.

- The O2 centre in London's Finchley Road, the first circular YO! Sushi.

- In the Millennium Dome.

- In the food halls of both Selfridges and Harvey Nichols department stores.

- In Clerkenwell on Farringdon Road, the biggest yet with YO! Below and centre for our event catering and delivery business.

- Behind The London Eye at County Hall.

- In Sainsbury's supermarkets around the UK.

- Yo! to Go will deliver to you or cater a Yo! Event complete with portable conveyor.

- More Yo! Sushi restaurants and Yo! Below bars are opening all the time.